*the ultimate*

# POLITICS AND HISTORY QUIZ

*the ultimate*

# POLITICS
# AND
# HISTORY
# QUIZ

Tim Bourke
William Scally

Tara PRESS

*The Ultimate Politics and History Quiz*
First edition published by
Littlemore Press, Dublin, 2021

Second edition published by
Tara Press, Dublin 2022
www.TaraPress.net

ISBN 978-0-9545620-5-2

Images: *Adobe Photo Stock*

# Table of Contents

# Introduction

In the dark days of Covid time, confined to quarters in lockdown, the authors, William Scally and Tim Bourke retained their sanity by engaging in what proved to be an all-engrossing contest: devising a complex and broad-reaching series of questions that would brighten the pandemic days. The result was a slim volume that made a fine debut title.

Later, during 2022, Bourke and Scally reviewed and fully revised the first edition, eliminating certain material and introducing some 230 brand new questions and solutions. This culminated in a second edition boasting a generous make-over, with a broad range of updated puzzles for the discerning reader.

*The Ultimate Politics and History Quiz* contains five hundred questions together with their solutions. The questions traverse the world of politics and history and offer the reader what could be described as a rather testing mental workout. Ireland is the main focus of the questions; Britain, Continental Europe and North America figure significantly.

Some of the quiz questions are relatively straightforward; many are quite thought-provoking, including a number that have more than one correct answer. Others are cryptic or constructed with a play on words – even knowledge of the alphabet would not go astray! They require some imagination and lateral thinking. The solutions, however, discreetly located at the back of the book, provide instant relief for the perplexed or mind-boggled.

*The Ultimate Politics and History Quiz* is for those who enjoy flexing their mental muscles. It is versatile and can be enjoyed by oneself or in the company of family and friends. However it is engaged with, it is guaranteed to provoke, frustrate, exercise, irritate, satisfy, please, and, above all, to provide fun and entertainment.

# How to

One number in brackets after the question indicates the number of letters in the answer;

A series of numbers indicates the number of letters in each word, if more than one word in the answer;

One number and an apostrophe indicates the traditional Irish name format, 1'3 as in: O'Dea.

*the ultimate*

# POLITICS AND HISTORY QUIZ

# SECTION ONE:
# QUESTIONS

# QUESTIONS
## 01-100

## 01-100

1.  Uneasy lies the head that wears a _____ . (5)

2.  Would Pat and Anne favour proper hare coursing, at least in the West? (8)

3.  First Irish Chancellor of an African University: a) Name? (5, 6, 1'5) b) Appointed by this post-independence President? (5, 7) c) Location? (5)

4.  Achieved highest office, but never elected a TD: same name as current conservative MP for Cheadle. (4, 8)

5.  Igloo? (3, 5, 5)

6.  Great saint brought warmth and comfort to the lost, trapped and bewildered, including in North Kildare. (7)

7.  In the past, _____ preceded Gregorian but later, Brandon followed _____ . (6)

8. Like an Odearest, well sprung by Sean Bourke? (6, 5)

9. Not Raúl Castro or Fidel, but now, further south, Xiomara in _____ (8)

10. This Teuton proved to be great gas, for a while, anyway (8 or 9).

11. In Central Europe, would you vote for this party or ban it (6).

12. Burgesses: one traitor and one patriot (3, 5).

13. "Denmark's greatest philosopher"? (11)

14. Was this Chinese leader a heavy user of Wrigley's gum? (4, 2, 3)

15. Was he brought to heel at Troy? (8)

16. He seems to bloom in the Seanad. (5, 6)

17. Rosencrantz and Guildenstern at play. (6)

18. Political "co-habitation"(1997). (7, 6) and (6, 6).

19. Prime Minister once seen as a liberalising reformer, but now signs of ethnic and nationalist mode. (4)

20. In the long run, we are all dead. (4, 7, 6)

21. Once called certain French events "a permanent coup d'état"; later served himself in top position for 14 years. (10).

22. _____ Gray (nowadays), and Lady ____ Grey (rather then) could not be branded as Jesuits. (3) and (4).

23. This Society of Jesus member was shunned by most, if not all of his confreres, while visiting Milltown Park in the early 50s and was the author of a philosophical work which proved to have almost perennial appeal: a) Name him (8, 2, 7) (b) Name the philosophical work (3, 10, 2, 3)

24. Odd one out: George Shultz, David Owen, Hillary Clinton, Alexander Haig, Brian Lenihan (Senior), Dominic Raab, Madeleine Albright, Micheál Martin, Henry Kissinger? (7, 6).

25. This Russian has no peers in Siberia. (4, 7)

26. A briar pipe: he used this to charm and, arguably, deceive a nation! (6, 6)

27. Che Guevara, in seeking to export his political ideas, was captured and executed in this country? (7)

28. Who won the Meath by-election of 1875? Surname only? (7)

29. "Algérie Française" (1958), but *plus tard* not for these people. (6) and (5, 5).

30. "The barbers are open in _____ " Dáil remark June 2020. (7)

31. In the Cliveden set, it sounds like he was for, not against, this noxious emission. (4, 7)

32. This long serving Paraguayan dictator/general was not a nice lad! (10)

33. He was even more French than De Gaulle (by the sound of him). (6, 6-6)

34. Surname of predecessor of Castro (Fidel). (7)

35. Would not be in line for this decoration! (2): Eamon de ____, Maurice ____ de Murville.

36. Get a political party: (4, 4) _____ Maitlis; _____ Emerson; _____ Oakeshott; Fergus _____ ; _____ Harris; _____ Kerrigan; _____ Pierce; _____ Kuenssberg.

37. To be frank about it, knighted and later stripped – in art, he 'kept' very well under the circumstances. (7, 5)

38. Still around, not a real queen herself, and not Pearse. (6)

39. Was she or is she a left wing Bourbon in disguise? (8, 5)

40. Athlone politician and Chinese rebellion. (5)

41. More Dunganstown than Castleross. (3, 8)

42. Was his masterpiece belligerent or pacific or indeed both? (3, 7)

43. He put an astronomical effort into his prosecution of the defendant in the Monica Lewinsky affair. (7, 5)

44. What kind of headgear were these two wearing, by the sound of them? (7, 4)

45. His scratch on a Cabra Bridge led to a technology revolution. (7, 5, 8)

46. Past VP is part of l.s.d. (5)

47. What was the (Irish) surname of the founder of the Argentine navy? (5).

48. This quartet of 'horsemen' tried to do us proud. (5, 7, 1'5, 8)

49. Capital of Uruguay? (10)

50. An oft-quoted existentialist question? (2, 2, 2, 3, 2, 2)

51.  Odd man out, as never back in: Lynch, Cowen, Ahern, Kenny? (5)

52.  Once held in major IRA escapade, now in gyms, not shops. (3, 5)

53.  Capital of Paraguay? (8)

54.  Local lore had it, that he could reach the parish priest's doorbell in Cloyne with a puck of his sliotar, from 20 yards out. (7, 4)

55.  Archbishops of Dublin since John Charles McQuaid. (4, 8, 7, 6, 7)

56.  Big change up North in this constituency in 1983. (4, 7)

57.  One-time US presidential candidate, not a silver liquid! (9)

58.  Two former Norwegian Prime Ministers: one who served as head of an international organisation. (10) and one who currently serves as head of a different international organisation. (11)

59.  Entitled to self-nominate for next Irish presidential election. (8)

60.  Ministerial Helen close enough to Minister of State _____ , at least in constituency terms. (4)

61.　Did these upwardly mobile Irish-Americans in the 1980s bite the hand that fed them? (6, 9)

62.　This bird was quite feminine. (8, 7)

63.　After getting the top job, this "son of the manse" was caught in two minds, apparently. (6, 5)

64.　One time Norwegian Foreign Minister and UN Secretary-General: always understood the truth! (6 3)

65.　Was this global diplomat too big for his boots? (7, 7, 5)

66.　Down here Cormac is now in: up North a long time ago it was Joe and later　Bernadette and Paddy. (6)

67.　"We have declared for an Irish Republic, and will　live under no other law." Not Jack, but who said it? (4, 5)

68.　Before: _____ Paisley; _____ Robinson; _____ Foster.  Outcome is:  research, analysis, information, diary. (3)

69.　Two missing: Varadkar, Kenny, Bruton, Dukes, Fitzgerald, Cosgrave, Costello. (6, 6)

70.　Noted for her caviar? (6, 8)

71. Did this major US clean-sweeping politician operate in a vacuum? (7, 6)

72. Eisenhower, Kennedy, Johnson, Nixon, Carter, Reagan, Bush(Snr). Who is missing within that sequence? (4)

73. First female leader of an Irish political party (1937-1950). (8 7)

74. "Juan's gal". (5)

75. A very provincial dwelling. (8, 5)

76. Did this Italian take the biscuit? (9)

77. Was this a job for the Roncalli and Pacelli boys? (4)

78. One common factor at least: Ferris; Vincent P.; O'Donoghue; Catherine; Cullen; Mansergh; Michael; Heydon; Kenny. (6)

79. Chamberlain; Churchill; Attlee; Churchill; MacMillan;Douglas-Home;Wilson;Heath;Wilson; Callaghan. Who is missing from the sequence? (4)

80. Long serving Papal Nuncio to Ireland, (before the 1970s). (9)

81. "Ich bin ein Berliner." (4, 1, 7)

82. Was this academic also a locksmith? (5, 5)

83. Was he responsible for the betrayal of Christ in Leeson Street? (10)

84. Russia: tennis and politics; the same but different. (8)

85. One was king, another kaiser, and a third, tsar. Relatively speaking, what were they in common? (7)

86. At least in theory, he was in pursuit of justice. (4, 5)

87. AJF O'Reilly once suggested that the distinguishing feature of the Irish Co-Operative Movement was _____ . (3, 7, 2, 11)

88. Andreas and George: father and son; one-time Prime Ministers. a) Surname (10)  b) Country (6)

89. Did this Englishman revert to Down in his pursuit of a past colonial vision? (5, 6)

90. Major Irish office holders: G, then W, then another W, and then G again. Name G. (9)

91. There was Declan (then) and Patrick (now) and in between there was _____ . (3)

92. Who was the President of the European Commission that resigned en masse? (6)

93. In a part of Leinster, _____ is a T.D. (7)

94. Which three Presidents of the European Commission served more than one term. (9, 6, 7)

95. If Tet was the military game changer in Vietnam, this massacre was the public opinion one. (2, 3)

96. The over-arching US rationale informing the Vietnam war was known as _____ _____ _____ (3, 6, 6)

97. Who was the only British President of the European Commission? (7)

98. A strategic overview, from the Hellfire Club. (3, 8, 8)

99. The political and institutional structures underpinning the framework documents leading to the "Good Friday" (Belfast) Agreement. Strand 1; (8) Strand 2; (5-5) Strand 3. (4-4)

100. This Saorstát Minister reduced the old age pension from 10 shillings to 9 shillings a week. (6, 6)

# QUESTIONS
## 101-200

## 101-200

101. *Fides et ratio*: papal encyclical. Author?
(4, 4, 2)

102. Not John Rawls, this tract proved influential for a time in some party circles here. (7, 1, 4, 7)

103. As Eugene O'Neill almost put it, "cometh the hour, cometh the _____ " (6)

104. Lawyer, office holder in Irish politics and academic who wrote robustly about the Constitution. (4, 5)

105. Did this tradesman flee the Hunt in the U.K. in July 2022? (4, 3)

106. Widely regarded as Germany's greatest thinker/ writer? (6)

107. Who's afraid of her ? (8, 5)

108. This game for ruffians knew no boundaries. (5)

109. Ironically, many thought he fell short. (3, 4, 6)

110. An Abrahamic trio. (7, 12, 5)

111. He was often at large. (3, 3, 6)

112. Which three countries joined the EEC first after the original six member states (6-7, 7, 7)

113. There was the "beef" between these two guys. (8, 1'6)

114. Which three countries joined the EEC in the 1980s? (6, 5, 8)

115. Political contests in 2022: a) Truss v ------- (5) b) Le Pen v _____(6) c) Ruto v _____ (6)

116. A porcine view to rival Naples or San Francisco. (3, 3, 2, 4)

117. In Malta, in the 1950s and 1960s, Archbishop _____ (5) and Dom _____(7) of the Labour Party rather fell out.

118. Was he ahead of his Times? (7, 6)

119. UK exiled Archbishop _____ (8) from Cyprus in the 1950s.

120. This chap seemed to be chained to his office for an age. (5, 5)

121. It was said to be the year of the French, but at the end of the day, they really were not at these races. (9)

122. This country ' sounds' fishy. (7)

123. What is the official name of the Mormon religion? (3, 6, 2, 5, 6, 2, 6, -3, 6)

124. A fox could make his sign in this country (7)

125. It can be argued of this renowned Irish institution that, by and large, it took the King's shilling. (7's, 10)

126. Philosopher and economist, neo-classical, a rival to Keynes. (9, 3, 5)

127. This Irish civil servant of old, sounded like she enjoyed a pint. (6, 5)

128. Was he the first man of Israel? (5, 3, 6)

129. This man from the South Circular Road area in Dublin was in his time a successor of Moses. (5, 6)

130. Political comedies: Scrap_____ (8) Spitting _____ (5) Callan's _____ (5)

131. This porcine, literary, and indeed political creature had grand military ambitions. (8)

132. Which grandson of Sigmund Freud, became a world famous painter? (6)

133. He sailed as if on a cloud. (6, 5)

134. Name changes, politics and culture:
a) Bombay _____ (6) b) St. Petersburg _____ (9)
c) _____ (9), then Constantinople and later _____ (8)

135. These "Postmen" were kept going by a sore throat. (8, 9)

136. Name changes, Irish variations:
Maryborough _____ (10) Rath Luirc _____ (11) An Uaimh _____ (5)

137. Features of pre-Communist China: a) it was more than an average hike (3, 4, 5)  b) this would have been beyond the capacities of the combined CIF membership. (3, 5, 4)

138. Who coined the phrase "false consciousness"? (4, 4)

139. "It's like being savaged by a dead sheep". Who said this? (5, 6)  About whom? (8, 4)

140. A Crown Court now sits in this former "priest ridden" town. (7)

141. Now Communist Beijing's political and ceremonial centrepiece (3, 5, 4, 2, 3, 6)

142. "Spy politics": *shaken and not stirred.* (5, 4)

143. "My name is Ozymandias, King of Kings, look on my works ye mighty and _____"(7)

144. Relic in this city has been shrouded in mystery. (5)

145. Past comedies: a) "That was the _____ that was". (4) b) _____ Pictorial Weekly. (5)

146. Russia: "practical truth ". (6)

147. Like Pope Leo XIII, this European was a champion of subsidiaries. (7, 6)

148. Labour MP married to former Prime Minister of which country? (7)

149. The derogatory name the US military used for the Vietnamese enemy. (5)

150. John McCain et al "resided" in this POW camp, widely known as _____ _____ _____ . (3, 5, 6)

151. All northern rock(s) (one inanimate, two human):
a) Ailsa _____ off the West coast of Scotland
(5) b) Not quite a Carson (5) c) Not quite a
James (7)

152. Sometime in the future, will she be thinking of
Ramsay? (4, 3)

153. The Soviet, or perhaps the Irish, "green"
movement. (8)

154. One time Prime Minister of Finland: moved on, but
not to the "Gazette". (5)

155. A pressing matter: a) several centuries ago;
(3, 9, 8, 5) b) A far later British copycat. (9).

156. The principle of subsidiarity was more or less
mooted in this Papal Encyclical. (In Latin; 5, 7)

157. In what local election out East in 2022 was the
total electorate some 150 million people? (5, 7)

158. Party leaders: Fitt; Hume; Ritchie; Eastwood
a) Which party? (initials only, 4)
b) Which two past party leaders are missing
(6 and 9)

159. "It's the economy, stupid!" Who coined this
phrase? (5, 8)

160. This directory of the realm, has a Russian entry. (5's  7)

161. Unlike Saul of Tarsus, he does not seem to have had a Damascene conversion. (6, 2, 5)

162. It was not to be the Garden of Eden. (4, 5)

163. "Vive le _____ Libre!"   (De Gaulle 1967) (6)

164. Powerful political figures in Brazil and the Philippines respectively; "customary form of address". (4 and 8)

165. This political leader (still around), popularised *Bunga Bunga* "evenings". (6, 10)

166. Archbishop of Canterbury who crowned Elizabeth II in 1953. (6)

167. This north western Syrian port city on the Mediterranean and its hinterland is Al-Assad's home base. (7)

168. The name of Al-Assad's minority Shia sect is _____ ? (7)

169. This Academy sounds like an Italian river. (8, 2)

170. A grander version of the IPA. (5, 9, 1'14)

171. A University founded under Royal Charter in 1592. (7, 7, 6)

172. Was this a "method of indoctrination" before its time? (3, 8, 2, 10)

173. From a French viewpoint, was this the end of the world? (10)

174. This Antipodean was more than birdlike, in or out of office. (3,5)

175. The model T gave rise to this 'ism'. (7)

176. In Oberammergau, Germany, what is the production that the locals put on every decade in the public square'? (3, 7, 4)

177. Directed by Visconti, with music by Mahler and Bogarde as the leading man. Name the film. (5, 2, 6)

178. Is it easy to fall in this African capital? (7)

179. Some 30 years ago, who said "Well Mr. Collins, tell us (the Speaker's Cabinet) how you (the EU) propose to solve our problems". (1, 1, 2, 5)

180. Somewhat like a quantum physics puzzle, this College is both in Cambridge and not in Cambridge. (7)

181. Pride of Grecian antiquity, looted by the British, known as: (3, 5, 7)

182. Michael and Mattie very much still there, but _____ has gone. (6)

183. Which Irish Dáil constituency has three grass race tracks. (9)

184. The bones of early Roman Christians lie here. (3, 9)

185. He was 'King of the Castle' for a long time, but well north west of Monaghan. (4, 6)

186. Irish politician who tasted a variety of exotic leaves in his day. (5, 5)

187. Some 30 years ago, his swansong in U.K politics was on late Irish telly? (5, 6)

188. Name three past Presidents of the Irish Farmer's Association, who were elected members of the European Parliament. (6, 4, 5)

189. Two Labour members were elected to the European Parliament from the same constituency in Ireland: a) In what year? (4) b) From which constituency? (6) c) Name them. (O'7 and O'5)

190. Irish think-tanks most unlikely to be doing what the answer does! (3) ESR _____ ; TAS _____ ; IIE _____ .

191. This Sri Lankan sounding cop (who always got his man) was the worst dressed 'star' in TV history. (7)

192. One of seven siblings from a small farm holding in Co. Cork, who became leader of Ireland's second largest farmer representative organisation. (5, 7)

193. Which Taoiseach during his period of office was involved with four different Presidents? (8)

194. Which President during his periods of office was involved with four different Taoisigh? (7)

195. Irish Social History, Radio Eireann (1950s and 1960s): a) "Question Time" was hosted by: (3, 7) b) "Take the Floor" was hosted by: (3, 3) c) Complete: "The Kennedys of: --------------".(10)

196. This State is foreign in America. (3, 5, 10)

197. Boys from Drimnagh who climbed to the top of the political ladder? (5, 3)

198. Even Hamburgers agree that this is the paper of record. (11, 10, 7)

199. Myth has it that an apple falling on his head from a tree under which he was reading, triggered a new law of physics. What law? (7) Name of scientist? (6)

200. This Pole was regarded as the first modern astrophysicist. (10)

# QUESTIONS
## 201-300

# ?

## 201-300

201. Posted up North. (7, 4, 6)

202. Irish Social History, Radio Telefís Eireann (1960s). Name the presenters: "Jackpot" (3, 5 and 5, 5) b ) "Quicksilver" (5  4)

203. Celtic propaganda? (3, 5, 4)

204. "Lord, make me pure, but not yet." To whom is this aspiration attributed? (2, 9)

205. Five proofs for the existence of God.  Who formulated them? (2, 6, 7)

206. He "christianised" Rome. (11)

207. He succeeded Adenauer. (6, 6)

208. Relatively speaking, this scientist is peerless (8)

209. Across the Cork-Kerry  mountains,  this pass confirmed  that the royal writ was well represented in the new Irish state. (3, 5, 4)

210. You can't hold the Easter candle to him. (7, 7)

211. In what Canadian province is the city of London. (7)

212. He wrote this economic treatise without the help of Eve. The book (3, 6, 2, 7); the author. (4, 5)

213. This Shannonside lad, was a tribune all unto himself. (7, 6)

214. In a Jubilee message in 2022 to Britain's Queen Elizabeth, who said: "You are the golden thread that binds our two countries" (8, 6)

215. This magazine had a weekly satirical column by "Denis" on life with "Margaret". (7, 3) What was the name of the weekly column in question? (4, 4)

216. RTE commentator on the funeral of JFK (7, 1'5)

217. The longest-serving broadcaster in RTE (4, 6)

218. Who wrote: a) *History of the Department of Finance up to 1958* (5, 7) b ) *The Government and Politics of Ireland* (5, 5)

219. Was this former Prime Minister of Canada the son of a lord by the sound of him? (6,7)

220. This leading Nazi was the recording secretary at the notorious "final solution" Wansee Conference (5, 8)

221. In England, the June 2022 by-elections in Honiton and Tiverton, and Wakefield took place exactly six years after what political event? The _____ (6) _____ (10)

222. Key Nazi leader assassinated in Czechoslovakia in 1942. (8, 8)

223. Chinese philosopher of great significance. (9)

224. Well known historical political figures and modern political journalists. Match them with their appropriate forenames:
O'Connell: _____ _____ (6, 4)
Connolly: _____ _____ (5, 4)
Wilson: _____ _____ (6, 4)

225. The political governance concept of "the Aireacht" made its debut in this late-sixties reform proposal. (3, 6, 6)

226. Franco's remains were recently disinterred from this memorial site. (3, 6, 2, 3, 6)

227. Back in the day, a Donegal Ceann Comhairle. (6, 7)

228. He was born in South America, but largely raised in the Co. Wexford family castle. Name? (5, 2, 5) Castle? (5)

229. These "yellow-bellies" from the past could play senior hurling. (3, 8)

230. Became a well-known, indeed famous building associate of Bertie's. (5, 3, 9)

231. Assassinated: _____ Lumumba; _____ Palme; Leon, _____; _____ Franz Ferdinand; Abraham _____ .
Then get a major political philosopher. (5)

232. On interest rates, in summer 2022, this pair were of great interest (and still are).
(9, 7 and 6, 4)

233. Although he was on the rocks towards the end, he made the bay his own. (4, 6)

234. Were his hands tied during the Falklands war? (4, 4)

235. Two Olivers went head to head. One lost his in London, the other is on display in what part of Ireland? (8)

236. He wrote a letter home every week. (8, 5)

237. Michael Mills, David Thornley, Michael McInerney, among others, did not play this game, but were participants, nonetheless. (3, 7, 2, 3, 5)

238. A doctor in charge in the House, in his day. (4, 1'6)

239. "Every Prime Minister needs a Willie." To whom was Margaret Thatcher referring? (6, 8)

240. Which leading US politician, now the junior Senator from Utah, is a Mormon? (4, 6)

241. She was the only public figure of her sex to officially greet JFK in Ireland. (7, 7)

242. She was the first woman to contest a constitutional case on contraception in Ireland. It became known as the _____ case. (5)

243. Scottish leader of a Labour Party in his day. (5, 8)

244. When he got stranded, had he a case to answer? (5, 8)

245. Seoirse Beag O Cymru? (5, 6)

246. Was Pakistan's capital, from "independence" to the mid-eighties. (7)

247. Who managed Wexford to its last All-Ireland in the late 1990s. (4 7)

248. Bangladesh, formerly known (post independence) as _____ . (4, 8)

249. Regarded as one of the first modern books on elections; in this case the 1960 US presidential election: a) the book. (3, 6, 2, 3, 9); b) the author. (8, 1, 5)

250. He was the 'John Charles McQuaid' of Melbourne back in the day. (10, 6)

251. This Killane boy was wanted in Australia for disturbing the peace. (3, 5)

252. This Wicklow-man from a Church of Ireland background became President of the GAA. (4, 8)

253. The major European powers conference in 1881 to divide up Africa, was held in this city. (6)

254. "The fools! The fools, they have left us our Fenian dead, and Ireland unfree shall never be at peace." Who was the orator? (7, 6)

255. US Senator; democratic party (West Virginia), was a key negotiator and voter in the Senate in 2021 and 2022. Name. (3, 7)

256. Cork GAA star, with equal facility in both codes, (5, 5-6).

257. Neil Kinnock's Welsh political inspiration. (7, 5)

258. This former MLA was not at Trafalgar. (6, 10)

259. Conor's book on Kitty's boyfriend? (7, 3, 3, 5)

260. From his continental base, with what aid did Joyce map Dublin's streets and places accurately? (5, 9)

261. This Tammany Hall demagogue was not selected for the All-Ireland final. (4, 6)

262. He was the first catholic candidate in a US presidential election. (2, 5)

263. An 'Irish' city in old Montana! (5)

264. He got a job, out of the blue, in Foreign Affairs, but he stayed in the same House. (3, 5)

265. This Anglo-French agreement after World War I neatly produced two new "desert" states. (5, 5)

266. Which Greek classic do Bloom's wanderings in Dublin represent. (3, 7)

267. She was the first black US ambassador. (7, 6, 5)

268. Authors:  a) *The Country Girls* (4, 1'5).
b) Was he a "Quare Fellow"? (7, 5)
c) He was at home *Amongst Women* (4, 8)

269. Murderer/assassin in the theatre. (4, 6, 5)

270. Murdered/assassinated in the cathedral. (6, 1, 6)

271. Dedicated to (failed) assassination attempts on Charles de Gaulle. Nickname? (3, 6)

272. *The Third Man*, who was a master of this and other spy novels and film screenplays? (6, 6)

273. On "The Dead" from Joyce's *Dubliners*:
a) who (when terminally ill) directed the film? (4, 6)
b) the townhouse in the book was located on which Dublin quay? (6, 6)
c) who played the Irish tenor who entertained the dinner party? (5, 9)

274. Was she a charitable mother? (4, 9)

275. Did this abstemious Dubliner go a bridge too far? (4, 6)

276. Had a Damascene about turn ? (5, 4)

277. Despite central heating, double-glazing etc., it sounds a very "draughty" place. (8)

278.    Better than Perrier or Pellegrino? (7, 5)

279.    Directed by Orson Welles, this film often
        critically, if not widely, regarded as the greatest
        film ever made. (7, 4)

280.    A Doctor's son from Hispaniola.
        (4, 3, 8)

281.    This chap was head of the Dominicans, over half
        a century ago. (6, 8)

282.    Well known Australian political strategist for
        hire has been widely associated over the years
        with the Conservative Party in the UK. (6, 6)

283.    Name three Ulster cardinals since the 1970s.
        (7, 4, 5)

284.    Had he blood on his hands and on his feet? (5, 3)

285.    This man founded a lay organisation modelled
        on Roman military structures. (5, 4)

286.    Four large Irish lakes: Get a currency first and
        follow with the name of a US Senator. (4, 4)

287.    In Pakistan, his pitch for a prospective second
        innings is (or was) that "It's just not cricket"!
        (5, 4)

288. In Ireland close friends with a mix of political, academic, and theological interests; one died in 2011, the other in 2021. (10, 8)

289. What tax was brought in by the Fine Gael-Labour government in the 1970s and later abolished by Fianna Fail? The _____ tax? (6)

290. GBS and the Webb-Ellis's were founder members of this group. (3, 6, 7)

291. This German introduced social policy to modern governance. (8)

292. Name the politician who sponsored and led the debate on the succession legislation (Succession Act) in Ireland in the 1960s. (7)

293. Former country names:
Ghana (4, 5)
Sri Lanka (6) Ethiopia (9)

294. John Reidy wrote the ground-breaking score for this film. (4, 4)

295. The Irishman who wrote the book/screenplay for this *Longest Day*? (9, 4)

296. This coastal country associated with French colonial elephant tusks. (4, 7)

297. In the Indian Ocean, in unity for a long time with the "home country"! (7)

298. Henry Kenny's Fianna Fáil football counterpart? (4, 8)

299. What additional name does this Donegal politician have? (3, 4)

300. Came full belt on to the yellowbellies, and later to Europe. (5, 5)

# QUESTIONS
## 301-400

## 301-400

301. This TD (deceased) played a hurling and football final in Croke Park on the same day. (3, 5)

302. "There was a sound of revelry by night, and _____ capital had gathered then her beauty and her chivalry": a) What country? (7) b) Before what battle? (8)

303. Name the three Presidents of Sinn Fein since 1970. (1'8, 5, 8)

304. Who said to an Arizona election official in November 2020: "We've got lots of theories. We just don't have the evidence"? (4, 8)

305. Who was the defeated candidate in the 2020 leadership contest in the Green Party in Ireland? (9, 6)

306. What election contraption was this 'snowman' famous for? (3, 11)

307. Who said: "How can you govern a country that has 246 varieties of cheese"? (7, 2, 6)

308. What 'treatise' was the main intellectual influence on Arthur Griffith, the founder of the original Sinn Fein? (3, 12, 2, 7)

309. In more recent times, what was the nickname of the Sinn Fein/IRA 'insider' who was a secret agent of the British security forces? (10)

310. Loyalists could not, at one point, beat a single drum on this road. (8)

311. Nothing to do with Atlanta or Tbilisi but centre stage with the Brothers of Italy (7, 6)

312. Who was a) Special Counsel to Richard Nixon in the Watergate era? (4, 4), b) Attorney-General during Nixon's Presidency? (4, 8)

313. Two former UK Prime Ministers: Match with these two constituencies. Sedgefield (5), Huntingdon. (5)

314. In the political comedy/drama, "Yes Minister", complete the names of two of the main characters:
a) Jim _____ (6)
b) Sir _____ Appleby. (8)

315. Two fathers and sons, some two centuries apart, served as Presidents of the United States. Surnames only. (5, 4)

316. Elected president of large country in 2012, and did not survive, even with codes! (5)

317. At least one common experience of office in Ireland: MN, BL, C McC, RQ, R McS, AD, GC, but never _____ (9)

318. A traditional mode: Sweden, Spain, United Kingdom, Norway, Netherlands, Denmark: a) The mode? (8) and b) add an appropriate European country. (7)

319. Robert and Hillary were once elected in _____ for a new beginning. (3, 4)

320. Who is the "teddy bear" named after? (8, 9)

321. With what sweets did Ronald Reagan eat his way through cabinet meetings? (10)

322. Sons-in-law and daughter-in-law also held political office; outcome is a very important court:
Sean Lemass: _____
Garret FitzGerald: _____
Michael Pat Murphy: _____ (3)

323. Once Parliamentary Secretaries and all Ireland football medallists: sons achieved higher office. (5, 6)

324. _____ liver salts still in stock in Dublin! (7)

325. Brothers: get the Surnames.
a) Robert ("Robin") was an MP and UK government Minister and James was the penultimate Prime Minister of Northern Ireland (10, 5) b) David and Ed; in this century, both members of Labour cabinets and leadership rivals. (8)

326. Stalin: a) Daughter: first name; (8) b) Lead military commander: surname? (6) c) Stalin's successor: first name and surname? (6, 8)

327. Churchill: a) Son; (8) b) Wife; (10) c) Childhood residence; (8, 6) d) Adult residence? (9)

328. This Greek philosopher drank himself to death. (8)

329. Eliminated: outcome is a post-war Belgian prime minister and European and international statesman: _____ Laval,_____ Sadat, _____ O'Higgins, _____ Allende, _____ Lincoln. (5)

330. The Spandau Two? (4, 5)

331. "Start packing _____, the Kennedys are coming" (1960 campaign) (5).

332. *To Katanga and Back*; carefully constructed or blunder (Initials only)? (1, 1, 1,'1)

333. In the late 20th century, Clonmel "Ceann", and not uair amhain. (6)

334. Vietnam War: a) the changing offensive; (3) b) the North Vietnamese army chief. (4)

335. The French imperial project came to an end at this battle. (4, 4, 3)

336. No mercy at (Paris) Versailles, merely water! (10)

337. British Islands by choice and name, but not for all. Is there some bad wine in their other name? (8)

338. One time Chancellors of the Exchequer; Churchill, Gaitskell, MacMillan, Callaghan: who is the odd man out? (9)

339. One time green policing in north Dublin. (7)

340. What does Abuja have in common with Brasilia? (8)

341. Was he a violinist in Rome's olden days? (4)

342. Father and Son; one President of the Executive Council of the Irish Free State; one Taoiseach. (8)

343. Away out East, was he a case of calling the kettle black? (3, 3)

344. "Was this Iberian judicial process unduly inquisitive? (3, 7, 11)

345. One-time US Secretary of State could work in the dark! (8)

346. One-time members of the Dáil: Johnny, Billy, Mildred. (3)

347. This "red army" excelled in urban-rural re-alignment. (5, 5)

348. Labour's Churchill? (6, 5)

349. Recently deceased spy writer under this *nom-de-plume*. (4, 2, 5)

350. Now the FSB, before that the KGB and before that the NKVD, but what preceded these three? (3, 5)

351. Tully may have ducked in time, but this prominent leader had no chance. (5, 5)

352. Was this "foreigner" noted for mixing his drinks? (7)

353. Before her elevation in 2017, immigrants and security kept her busy, if not praying to the Little Flower. (3)

354. "Labour owed more to Methodism than to Marx". Who proposed this idea? (5, 6)

355. "Treaties are like girls and roses; they last while they last." (2, 6)

356. The Islamic tradition that holds the Saudi system together is called _____ ? (9)

357. Father and child (past and present): get an Irish political party (4): a) John A and _____ Costello, b) _____ and Beverley Flynn, c) Dan and Dick _____ , d) Sean and Noel _____ .

358. Suffragette at Epsom Derby in 2013; Irish Ombudsman to European Ombudsman (2013) (5)

359. A common experience of high political office: but one did not ever hold the same senior ministry as the others did. EK, BC, BA, JB, AR, CH. (2)

360. Author of: a) *The Great Hunger*. (5, 7-5) and
b) *Ireland since the Famine*"?
(1, 1, 1, 5)

361. Did Tim Pat Coogan's mother blow this up?
(3, 3, 4)

362. An Orwellian quintet:
a) Did he pay "Homage" to this place? (9)
b) Tyranny in a rural setting? (6, 4)
c) Was this work out of date? (4)
d) The road to here was definitely not en route
to a seaside resort (5, 4) and
e) A tale of two cities. (6, 3, 5)

363. Father and daughter were simultaneously
members of Dáil Éireann. Surname? (5)

364. In the original spy/political thriller *The Ipcress File*:
a) What actor played Harry Palmer? (7, 5)
b) What character was the main "bad guy"? (5)

365. Brother and sister, at times both Ministers,
were members of Dail Eireann at the same time
for a number of years. Surnames? (7, 7)

366. Four Presidents or Prime Ministers in the past,
beginning with "De" as separate word and then?
(6, 7, 6, 5)

367. Following a referendum in May 1944: Which northern European country became an independent republic in 1944? (7) With which country had it been linked with since 1814? (7)

368. In the Danish political drama "Borgen" (2022, 4th series), the central character _____ _____ plays the role of Foreign Minister. (8 6)

369. In the 2020 Irish general election, which two constituencies did not return any FF or FG deputies? (9-6) and (6, 5-7)

370. In 2020, in which constituency was no deputy elected, apart from FF and FG? (4, 5-4)

371. Which organisation introduced the first major employee share ownership scheme (ESOP) in Ireland? (7, 7)

372. Presidents: One past, one present, beginning with the letter Z. (4, 8)

373. Who was General Secretary of the Irish Congress of Trade Unions (2001-2015), held a number of public appointments, and was also chief executive of a major charity? (5, 4)

374. Name the offshore oil/gas exploration vehicle created by A.J.F. O'Reilly some 40 years ago ? (8, 9)

375. Two "Sergei's" "up to their necks" in Ukraine. (6 and 6)

376. Two brothers: one Taoiseach and one a Minister at the same time. Surname? (6)

377. Foreign correspondents/journalists:
Sean _____ (RTE, 6) Orla _____ (BBC, 6)
Alex _____ (Sky, 8) Douglas _____ (France 24, 7)

378. High English legal officer also a master baker? (6, 2, 3, 5)

379. The White House in Africa! (10)

380. The development of the atomic bomb: a) name of project? (9)   b) director of project? (11) c) location of project, either specific or US State name? (3, 6)

381. Journalists in current affairs, politics etc. Get the missing names (below) and arrive at an African country (7).
Miriam _____ (4); _____ Burke-Kennedy (4);
_____ Mc Inerney (5); Miriam _____ (10):
_____ Prone(5); Niamh _____ (5); _____ Guerin (5)

382. A practising politician could well have chosen this 1992 Aintree Grand National winner! (5 8)

383. Elected past and present: New York, Kerry South, Cork North West; all the same? (8)

384. Across the water, they don't race inside it, but keep an eye on you, all the same. (1, 1, 1, 1, 10)

385. One could be struck down with a bug from this place in England. (6, 4)

386. Sounded like he cleaned up in America in days past. (1, 5, 6)

387. Elected President of Chile on two occasions, and now UN High Commissioner for Human Rights. (8, 8)

388. Formerly Formosa. (6)

389. Predecessor of Suharto. (7)

390. Daughter of Ali Bhutto (Muslim forename only). (7)

391. "In the state of nature, the life of man is solitary, poor, nasty, brutish and short." The answer is a social contract for an absolute sovereign. Name the political philosopher. (6, 6)

392. Last President of Ceylon. (12)

393. Who said a) "Eli Eli, Lama Sabachthani":
Believed to be the last words of _____ (5, 6)
b) Language/dialect ? (7)

394. Who wrote: a) "Home before Dark" and
"Home after Dark"? (4, 7)
b) "Uncle Vanya"? (5, 6)  c) "Dr Zhivago" (5, 9)
d) "Dancing at Lughnasa" ? (5, 5)

395. In Ireland, there have been nine referenda on
EU-related issues. How many were passed at the
first referendum on the issue presented? (4)

396. Who wrote biographies of:  a) both Sean Lemass
and Noel Browne; (4, 6) b) both John A. Costello
and Eamon de Valera? (5, 9)  c) of Patrick
Hillery? (4, 5) d) of Peter Sutherland? (4, 5)

397. The age of the youngest Catholic Pope (6)

398. Who said, on the occasion of the visit of
Pope Francis to Ireland in 2018 [that the time
had come], "for us to build a more mature
relationship between church and state in Ireland
– a new covenant for the 21st century". It would
be one "in which religion would be no longer at
the centre of our society, but in which it still has
an important place". (8)

399.   Who, in his St Patrick's Day address (1943), referring to the ideal Ireland we would have, and with references to, 'right living,' 'frugal comfort', 'cosy homesteads', 'the romping of sturdy children', 'the laughter of happy maidens', added, "the home, in short, of a people living the life that God desires that men should live"? (2, 6)

400.   Between the wars, this gave Poland access to the Baltic. (3, 6, 8)

# QUESTIONS
## 401-500

$\textcircled{?}$

# 401-500

401. Was this Fianna Fáil TD (retired for some years), a member of the Church of Scotland? (6, 4)

402. Did he have a spring in his step? (9, 6)

403. This Western European country made Christmas Day an official holiday, as late as 1958. (8)

404. A leading pantheist poet? (7, 10)

405. "Autumn, season of mists and mellow fruitfulness, close bosom friend of the maturing sun".
Who is the poet? (4, 5)

406. Not a Belfast-located academy, rather this academic location, east of the Bann, for what might have been euphemistically called political reasons. (9)

407. Did this Protestant roll out the barrel for the SDLP? (4, 6)

408. Who wrote:
The original; *The Ipcress File*? (3, 8)
*Where Eagles Dare*? (8, 7)

409. He had a dramatic escape from captivity, but was "hunted down" at Westminster. (5, 5)

410. He was an iconic 'loyalist' figure, who stood firm in a gale. (5, 6)

411. Now Russian, Kaliningrad was a German city of what name? (10)

412. What was capital of the "Federal Republic of West Germany"? (4)

413. Did this Italian-sounding work from 1957 make French cows more productive? (3, 6, 2, 4)

414. In 1967, Glasgow Celtic were certainly not of a mind for what would be named there some forty years later! (3, 6, 6)

415. Who was this corner's most enduring (and arguably most popular) speaker? (4, 6, 5), Location of corner within London? (4, 4)

416. Usually, but certainly not always, not a good London address for spendthrifts to reside in. (2, 7, 6)

417. "Let a hundred flowers blossom". This wish of Mao signified the start of: (3, 8, 10)

418. Did some people think some decades ago that this prominent Irish politician had taken out North Vietnamese citizenship? (6, 5)

419. Men wear veils and women do not among what African people, also known as "Blue Arabs"? (7 or 6) both are correct.

420. What was Mao's other big "transformational" initiative called? (3, 5, 4, 7)

421. A "tricky" and "wet" entrance some decades ago. (9)

422. Which sons were members of Dáil Éireann for some or all of the time when their father was Taoiseach? (6, 2, 6) and (6, 8) and (4, 6)

423. Havel and Klaus, more in common than a country or a Presidency. (6)

424. Who said in January 2021 "and the key thing is we've got our fish back. They're now British fish and they're better and happier fish for it." (5, 4-4)

425. Fianna Fáil got 77 seats in 1933, 1938, 1989, and in _____ . (4)

426. Powerful President of a European country: would he give an interview to RTE? (5, 6, 7)

427. When the Gardaí came to arrest Charles Haughey in 1970, what prominent public figure, it was said, was visiting his house? (5, 5)

428. This borderlands politician, who served as an Irish minister, was no relation of Brian.(7, 8)

429. Throughout the 1970s this was a morning RTE radio programme, that morphed into a two-hour radio show for the next two decades. What was it called ? (3, 3, 5, 4)

430. A _____ in Kildare South, and _____ in Cork South-West. (5, 5)

431. *Cast a cold eye on life and death*:
    a) on whose headstone? (5)
    b) Location of cemetery? (10)

432. Would you feel safe in Ireland with her, driving? (3, 1'7)

433. What is the Hebrew name for God? (6)

434. On July 6 2022, who _____ (7) said of whom _____(5 and 5) as "the first case of sinking ships leaving the rat"?

435. Reputedly, Cleopatra succumbed from this reptile's venomous bite. (3)

436. Sinn Féin got 37 seats in 2020, and Labour got 37 seats in _____ . (4)

437. Egyptian leaders, get the power in a neighbouring area: (5) _____ Fattah al-Sisi; Anwar _____; Gamal _____ Nasser; _____ Mubarak; Mohamed _____ .

438. A Rose in Mayo, but in Cavan-Monaghan it is _____ . (7)

439. Four major long running 'soaps' by RTE as follows: 1960s (5, 3); 1965-1979 (3, 8); Mid-eighties to early noughties (7); From 1989 onwards (4, 4)

440. This country was not ruled by a blacksmith. (8, 8)

441. He got his Irish sounding 'nickname' from his mother's side. After his death, this name gained worldwide iconic status. (3)

442. Did she have an Oscar in the 19th century? Known in literary circles as _____ . (8)

443. William and Michael _____ : an Upper House family. (5)

444. Nearly three centuries ago, he made "a modest proposal." (8, 5)

445. This Scots/Canadian economist and one time Ambassador to India was a critical voice in "affluent" America . (4, 7, 9)

446. A schism dating from A.D. 632. (5, 4)

447. The body of a former Italian Prime Minister was found in the boot of a car. (4, 4)

448. Who was the first male figure to appear on Radio Telifis Eireann ? (5 2 6)

449. Did he make some overture about "1812"? (11)

450. In 2022, which Irish minister and departmental secretary- general travelled to Dubai for business? (8 and 4)

451. Which British politician has, inside the last decade, been sacked from cabinet positions by three different British Prime Ministers? (7, 4)

452. Which two Irish judges resigned from a legal role in Dubai in 2022? (6, 5)

453. Who designed St. Paul's Cathedral in London? (11, 4)

454. Not the boys of Kilmichael, but from not too far away. (3, 5, 4)

455. Three Irish bishops who 'resigned' from office within the last 30 years: a) Wexford (8) b) Cloyne (5) c) Galway (5)

456. Some 50 years ago, she made a spectacle of him: a) Who was the subject? (10, 6) b) Who was the object? (8, 8)

457. How many US Presidents were assassinated?(4)

458. Austrian Chancellor assassinated in 1934 (8)

459. President of Sri Lanka in September 2022? (5, 14)

460. This man, reared in Galway, became infamous in his day; not really a bag of laughs. (7, 5)

461. "We in the House of Lords are never in touch with public opinion. That makes us a civilised body". (Drama) Author (5, 5)

462. This English journalist sounds like a peaceful man. (6, 6)

463. According to George Bernard Shaw, a) whose "other island" was Ireland? (4, 5), b) In what Dublin street did Shaw live in his early years? (5, 6)

464. He sounds like a relation of John Hume, but far from it. (4, 7-4)

465. With which historical figure, did Jacob Rees-Mogg compare the ousting of Boris Johnson? (6, 6)

466. Name the Northern Ireland Secretary (appointed July 2022), who described "as utter and absolute nonsense" a claim that when a Junior Minister in Northern Ireland some years previously he had asked an official" whether he needed a passport to go to Derry" (8, 4)

467. Is this knight of the realm averse to using cheques or credit cards? (3, 7, 4)

468. Newspaper headline (July 14, 2022): "PM for PM": (5, 8) for (5, 8)

469. His (British) broadcasting gravitas held the kingdom in thrall on great occasions of church and state. (7, 8)

470. Not Maud Gonne, or indeed Sean or Willie John, but a prominent modern political journalist and author. (3, 7)

471. These sons of Irish fathers were also chips off the old block: a) Academic politics (5, 7)

b) Newspaper ownership; (6, 2, 6)  c) Sports broadcasting. (4, 1'5)

472.  In Wexford, noted for battle, and a pungent taste for climbing? (7, 4)

473.  Who once said: "The seventies will be socialist"? (7, 6)

474.  Would you play bridge with _____ ? (5)

475.  French style bowling in fashion; where in Wexford? (10)

476.  Sought successfully to join NATO in 2022. (6 and 7)

477.  The white  smoke signalling the election of a pope,  billows from what building. (3, 7, 6)

478.  What is the gathering of papal electors called ? (8)

479.  Across the pond, while centuries old, these states are also "new": (4, 6, 9, 6)

480.  Who were the founding members and co-leaders of the Social Democrats in Ireland in 2015? (8, 6, 8)

481.  Which founding member of the Social Democrats, joined Fianna Fail, and later became a cabinet minister? (8)

482. Not Laurence in Dublin long ago and did not win in Canada in 2021. (4)

483. Originally elected as Fine Gael TDs, but later elected as Independents, and are sitting members (2022). Michael _____ (5) Peter _____ (11) Denis _____ (8)

484. Former Irish Times columnist more contrarian than Eamonn Dunphy!! (4, 6)

485. James Plunkett showed the Dublin of Larkin and Murphy in a very poor light. (8, 4)

486.  Herbert Morrison's grandson. (5, 9)

487.  Is this chap half mad? (6)

488. Malcolm McArthur had a "pilot's view" from this chap's residence. (7, 8)

489. She sounds like she was like a city chief, but was in fact a head of government. (5, 4)

490. If the French gave us the *chaise longue*, the Turks gave us this _____ ? (3, 7)

491. *Darkness Before Noon* author. (6, 8)

492.  The two African colonies of Portugal. (6, 10)

493. A long-time leading politician (CSU) in Bavaria from the 1950s to the 1980s. (5, 5, 7)

494. In all fairness – according to this literary masterpiece – one often, but not always, follows the other: a) the book (5, 3, 10) b) the author. (6, 10)

495. Name four Irish Presidents who served two full terms. (1'5), (2, 6), (7), (8)

496. Originally elected for a political party, but later elected as Independents, and are sitting members (2022): Mattie (FF) _____ (7). Noel (PDs) _____(8). Carol (SF) _____(5) Michael (Lab) _____(8)

497. Nine in a row to be indulged. (3, 5, 7)

498. Long-serving cardinal from the Philippines (from 1974) who at times had an active political involvement. (3)

499. Name a member of the Biden-appointed cabinet that begins with the letter Y; (6) with B; (7) with A; (6) and with W. (5)

500. Name six Taoisigh that did not represent Dublin constituencies. (6, 5, 5, 6, 8, 5)

# SECTION TWO: SOLUTIONS!

# SOLUTIONS

## 01-100

# Solutions: 01-100

1. 'Crown'

2. Rabbitte

3. a) Conor Cruise O'Brien  b) Kwame Nkrumah
   c) Accra

4. Mary Robinson

5. The White House

6. Bernard

7. Julian

8. George Blake

9. Honduras

10. Schroeder or Schröder

11. Fidesz

12. Guy, Niall

13. Kierkegaard

14. Chou en Lai

15. Achilles

16. David Norris

17. Hamlet

18. Jacques Chirac and Lionel Jospin

19. Modi

20. John Maynard Keynes

21. Mitterrand

22. Sue and Jane

23. Teilhard de Chardin,
    b)The Phenomenon of Man.

24. Micheál Martin: (all Foreign Ministers or
    equivalents: only Micheál Martin obtained the
    top executive job in his country)

25. Lord Lebedev

26. Harold Wilson

27. Bolivia

28. Parnell

29. Harkis and pieds-noirs

30. "Seville"

31. John Profumo

32. Stroessner

33. Pierre Mendes - France

34. Batista

35. VC (Victoria Cross!)

36. Fine Gael (Emily, Newton, Isabel, Finlay, Eoghan, Gene, Andrew, Laura)

37. Anthony Blunt

38. Regina

39. Ségolène Royal

40. 'Boxer'

41. The Kennedys

42. Leo Tolstoy

43. Kenneth Starr

44. Schmidt, Kohl

45. William Rowan Hamilton

46. Pence

47. Brown

48. Carey, Kennedy, O'Neill, Moynihan

49. Montevideo

50. "To be or not to be"

51. Cowen

52. Ben Dunne

53. Asunción

54. Christy Ring

55. Ryan; Mc Namara; Connell; Martin; Farrell

56. West Belfast

57. Goldwater

58. a) Brundtland  b) Stoltenberg

59. Robinson

60. Troy

61. Reagan Democrats

62. Ladybird Johnson

63. Gordon Brown

64. Trygve Lie

65. Boutros-Boutros Ghali

66. Devlin

67. Liam Lynch

68. IPA: (Ian, Peter, Arlene)

69. Noonan; Dillon

70. Nicola Sturgeon

71. Herbert Hoover

72. Ford

73. Margaret Buckley

74. Evita

75. Leinster House

76. Garibaldi

77. Pope

78. Martin: (either forename or surname of all nine politicians)

79. Eden

80. Alibrandi

81. John F. Kennedy

82. Basil Chubb

83. Caravaggio

84. Medvedev

85. Cousins

86. John Rawls

87. "The absence of co-operation".

88. a) Papandreou  b) Greece

89. Enoch Powell

90. Gallagher

91. Joe

92. Santer

93. Munster

94.  Hallstein, Delors, Barroso

95.  My Lai

96.  The domino effect

97.  Jenkins

98.  The Tallaght Strategy

99.  a) Internal  b) North-South  c) East-West

100. Ernest Blythe

# SOLUTIONS
## 101-200

# Solutions: 101-200

101. John Paul II

102. *Towards a Just Society*

103. Iceman

104. John Kelly

105. Liam Fox

106. Goethe

107. Virginia Woolf

108. Rugby

109. "The Long Fellow"

110. Judaism; Christianity; Islam

111. "The Big Fellow"

112. United Kingdom;  Ireland;  Denmark

113. Reynolds, O'Malley

114. Greece, Spain, Portugal

115. Sunak; Macron; Odinga

116. The Bay of Pigs

117. Gonzi and Mintoff

118. Douglas Gageby

119. Makarios

120. Alfie Byrne

121. Castlebar

122. Finland

123. The Church of Jesus Christ of Latter-Day Saints

124. Denmark

125. Grattan's Parliament

126. Friedrich von Hayek

127. Thekla Beere

128. David Ben Gurion

129. Chaim Herzog

130. Saturday; Image; Kicks

131. Napoleon

132. Lucien

133. Edward Heath

134. Mumbai; Leningrad; Byzantium; Istanbul

135. Woodward and Bernstein

136. Portlaoise; Charleville; Navan

137. a) The Long March  b) The Great Wall

138. Karl Marx

139. Denis Healey; Geoffrey Howe

140. Preston

141. The Great Hall of the People

142. James Bond

143. Despair

144. Turin

145. Week; Hall's

146. Pravda

147. Jacques Delors

148. Denmark

149. Gooks

150. The Hanoi Hilton

151. a) Craig  b) James  c) William

152. Mary Lou

153. Glasnost

154. Stubb

155. a.) The Gutenberg Printing Press  b) Gestetner

156. Rerum Novarum

157. Uttar Pradesh

158. a) SDLP  b) Durkan and McDonnell

159. James Carville

160. Burke's Peerage

161. Bashir al Assad

162. Suez canal

163. Québec

164. Lula and Bongbong

165. Silvio Berlusconi

166. Ramsay

167. Latakia

168. Alamite

169. Sciences Po

170. École Nationale d'Administration

171. Trinity College, Dublin

172. The Doctrine of Precedence

173. Finisterre

174. Bob Hawke

175. Fordism

176. The Passion Play

177. Death In Venice

178. Tripoli

179. F.W. de Klerk

180. Harvard

181. The Elgin Marbles

182. Finian

183. Tipperary

184. The Catacombs

185. Neil Blaney

186. Peter Barry

187. Peter Brooke

188. Gillis; Lane; Maher

189. a) 1979 b) Dublin c) O'Connell and O'Leary

190. CIA

191. Columbo

192. James O' Keeffe

193. Cosgrave

194. Hillery

195. a) Joe Linnane b) Din Joe c) Castleross

196. The State Department

197. Dukes, Cox

198. *Frankfurter Allgemeine Zeitung*

199. a) Gravity   b) Newton

200. Copernicus

# SOLUTIONS
## 201-300

# Solutions: 201-300

201. *Belfast News Letter*

202. a) Gay Byrne and Terry Wogan   b) Bunny Carr

203. *The Irish News*

204. St Augustine

205. St Thomas Aquinas

206. Constantine

207. Ludwig Erhard

208. Einstein

209. The Healy Pass

210. Paschal Donohoe

211. Ontario

212. a) *The Wealth of Nations* b) Adam Smith

213. Vincent Browne

214. Emmanuel Macron

215. *Private Eye*; "Dear Bill"

216. Michael O'Hehir

217. John Bowman

218. a) Ronan Fanning   b Basil Chubb

219. Lester Pearson

220. Adolf Eichmann

221. Brexit Referendum

222. Reinhard Heydrich

223. Confucius

224. Daniel, Hugh  James, Tony  Harold, Mary

225. *The Devlin Report*

226. The Valley of the Fallen

227. Cormac Breslin

228. a) Chris de Burgh b) Bargy

229. The Rackards

230. 'Paddy the Plasterer'

231. Plato: (Patrice, Olaf, Trotsky, Archduke, Lincoln)

232. Christine Lagarde and Philip Lane

233. Sean Loftus

234. John Nott (or Noel Dorr)

235. Drogheda

236. Alistair Cooke

237. The Hurlers on the ditch

238. Rory O'Hanlon

239. Willie Whitelaw

240. Mitt Romney

241. Frances Condell

242. McGee

243. James Connolly

244. Roger Casement

245. Lloyd George

246. Karachi

247. Liam Griffin

248. East Pakistan

249. a) *The Making of the President*
    b )Theodore H White

250. Archbishop Mannix

251. Ned Kelly

252. Jack Boothman

253. Berlin

254. Patrick Pearse

255. Joe Manchin

256. Jimmy Barry-Murphy

257. Aneurin Bevan

258. Nelson McCausland

259. *Parnell and his Party*

260. Thom's Directory

261. Boss Croker

262. Al Smith

263. Butte

264. Jim Dooge

265. Sykes/Picot

266. The Odyssey

267. Shirley Temple Black

268. a) Edna O'Brien  b) Brendan Behan
     c) John McGahern

269. John Wilkes Booth

270. Thomas à Becket

271. The Jackal

272. Graham Greene

273. a) John Huston, b) Usher's Island
     c) Frank Patterson

274. Mary Aikenhead

275. Matt Talbot

276. Saint Paul

277. Chequers

278. Lourdes Water

279. Citizen Kane

280. Papa Doc Duvalier

281. Rafael Trujillo

282. Lynton Crosby

283. O'Fiaich;  Daly;  Brady

284. Padre Pio

285. Frank Duff

286. Rand Paul
     (Ree, Allen, Neagh, Derg)

287. Imran Khan

288. Fitzgerald and McDonagh

289. Wealth

290. The Fabian Society

291. Bismarck

292. Haughey

293. Gold Coast; Ceylon; Abyssinia

# SOLUTIONS

## 301-400

# Solutions: 301-400

301. Des Foley

302. a) Belgium, b) Waterloo

303. O'Bradaigh, Adams, McDonald

304. Rudy Giuliani

305. Catherine Martin

306. The ' swingometer'

307. Charles de Gaulle

308. The Resurrection of Hungary

309. Stakeknife

310. Garvaghy

311. Georgia Meloni

312. a) John Dean, b) John Mitchell

313. Blair, Major

314. a) Hacker   b) Humphrey

315. Adams; Bush

316. Morsi

317. Taoiseach (all were at one time Ministers for Finance)

318. a) Monarchy   b) Belgium

319. New York

320. Theodore Roosevelt

321. Jellybeans

322. ECJ (Lemass, FitzGerald, Murphy ie. CHARLES Haughey, EITHNE FitzGerald, JOHN O'Donoghue)

323. Kenny and Spring

324. Andrews

325. a) Chichester-Clark   b) Miliband

326. a) Svetlana   b) Zhukov   c) Georgy Malenkov

327. a) Randolph   b) Clementine   c) Blenheim Palace
d) Chartwell

328. Socrates

329. Spaak (Pierre; Anwar; Kevin; Salvador; Abraham)

330. Hess, Speer

331. "Mamie"

332. C.C.O'B

333. Treacy

334. a) Tet  b) Giap

335. Dien Bien Phu

336. Clemenceau

337. Malvinas

338. Gaitskell (never became Prime Minister)

339. Sargent

340. Capitals

341. Nero

342. Cosgrave

343. Pol Pot

344. The Spanish Inquisition

345. Albright

346. Fox

347. Khmer Rouge

348. Ernest Bevin

349. John le Carré

350. The Cheka

351. Anwar Sadat

352. Molotov

353. May

354. Denis Healey

355. de Gaulle

356. Wahhabism

357. SDLP (Declan, Padraig, Spring, Lemass)

358. Emily

359. EK: was never Minister for Finance; all the others were earlier in their careers.

360. a) Cecil Woodham-Smith, b) F.S.L. Lyons

361.  *The Big Wind*

362.  a) Catalonia  b) Animal Farm  c) 1984
      d) Wigan Pier  e) London and Paris.

363.  Barry

364.  a) Michael Caine  b) Dalby

365.  Lenihan and O'Rourke

366.  Valera;  Gasperi;  Gaulle;  Klerk

367.  a) Iceland   b) Denmark

368.  Birgitte Nyborg

369.  Roscommon-Galway, Dublin South-Central

370.  Cork North-West

371.  Telecom Éireann

372.  Zuma, Zelensky

373.  David Begg

374.  Atlantic Resources

375.  Lavrov and Shoigu

376.  Bruton

377. a) Whelan  b) Guerin  c) Crawford  d) Herbert

378. Master of the Rolls

379. Casablanca

380. a) Manhattan  b) Oppenheimer  c) Los Alamos
or New Mexico

381. Lesotho: (Lord, Eoin, Sarah, O'Callaghan,
Terry, Horan, Orla)

382. Party politics

383. Moynihan

384. G.C.H.Q. Cheltenham

385. Porton Down

386. J. Edgar Hoover

387. Michelle Bachelet

388. Taiwan

389. Sukarno

390. Benazir

391. Thomas Hobbes

392. Bandaranaike

393. a) Jesus Christ  b) Aramaic

394. a) Hugh Leonard   b) Anton Chekov,
     c) Boris Pasternak   d) Brian Friel

395. Five

396. a) John Horgan  b) David  McCullagh
     c) John Walsh and d) John Walsh
     (two different people)

397. Twelve

398. Varadkar

399. de Valera

400. The Danzig Corridor

# SOLUTIONS

## 401-500

# Solutions: 401-500

401. Seamus Kirk

402. Alexander Dubcek

403. Scotland

404. William Wordsworth

405. John Keats

406. Coleraine

407. Ivan Cooper

408. Len Deighton, Alistair MacLean

409. Airey Neave

410. Gusty Spence

411. Konigsberg

412. Bonn

413. *The Treaty of Rome*

414. *The Lisbon Treaty*

415. a) Lord Donald Soper   b) Hyde Park

416. 11 Downing Street

417. The Cultural Revolution

418. Ruairi Quinn

419. Touareg or Tuareg

420. The Great Leap Forward

421. Watergate.

422. Vivion de Valera and Declan Costello and Noel Lemass.

423. Vaclav

424. Jacob Rees-Mogg

425. 1997

426. Recep Tayyip Erdogan

427. Brian Walsh

428. Padraig Faulkner

429. The Gay Byrne Hour

430. Berry, Holly

431. a) Yeats  b) Drumcliffe

432. Liz O'Donnell

433. Yahweh

434. Starmer, Sunak and Javid

435. Asp

436. 2011

437. Hamas (Abdel, Sadat, Abdel, Hosni, Morsi)

438. Heather

439. Tolka Row, The Riordans, Glenroe, Fair City

440. Southern Rhodesia

441. Che

442. Speranza

443. Yeats

444. Jonathan Swift

445. John Kenneth Galbraith

446. Sunni: Shia

447. Aldo Moro

448. Eamon de Valera

449. Tchaikovsky

450. Donnelly and Watt

451. Michael Gove

452. Clarke and Kelly

453. Christopher Wren

454. The Healy Raes

455. a) Cumiskey  b) Magee  c) Casey

456. a) Bernadette Devlin  b) Reginald Maudling

457. Four

458. Dollfuss

459. Ranil Wickremesinghe

460. William Joyce

461. Oscar Wilde

462. Jeremy Paxman

463. John Bull's; Synge Street

464. Alec Douglas-Home

465. Julius Caesar

466. Shailesh Vara

467. Sir William Cash

468. "Penny Mordaunt for Prime Minister"

469. Richard Dimbleby

470. Sam McBride

471. a) David Farrell  b) Vivion de Valera  c) Tony O'Hehir

472. Vinegar Hill

473. Brendan Corish

474. Trump

475. Boolavogue

476. Sweden and Finland

477. The Sistine Chapel

478. Conclave

479. York; Jersey; Hampshire; Mexico

480. Donnelly; Murphy; Shortall

481. Donnelly

482. Erin

483. Lowry; Fitzpatrick; Naughten

484. John Waters

485. *Strumpet City*

486. Peter Mandelson

487. Maduro

488. Patrick Connolly

489. Golda Meir

490. The ottoman

491. Arthur Koestler

492. Angola and Mozambique

493. Franz Josef Strauss

494. *Crime and Punishment*, Fyodor Dostoevsky

495. O'Kelly, De Valera, Hillery, McAleese

496. McGrath; Grealish; Nolan; McNamara

497. The First Fridays

498. Sin

499. Yellen; Blinken; Austen; Walsh

500. Martin; Kenny; Cowen; Bruton; Reynolds; Lynch

# Acknowledgments

This book of quizzes, which originated in the friendly fire exchanged between two friends over an eighteen month period, would never have seen the light of day without the help and encouragement of a number of people. We would like to thank them all.

From the beginning, Tony Brown grappled with many of the proposed questions, offering valued opinion on the difficulties or otherwise of the quiz.

Liam Murphy generously examined, in detail, much of the material and offered important critical evaluation.

Stephen Collins's wisdom, encouragement and sound advice helped in defining the boundaries.

Clare Tuohy, while venturing the opinion that the quiz was "a mind game between Bourke and Scally", was supportive from start to finish.

For this second edition, Jean Hanly assisted with valuable advice, especially on sales and marketing.

A number of friends, at different turning points, provided just the right company to keep us to the task. Perhaps, unwisely, we did not always accept recommendations or advice, but very much valued their interest and support. Muiris FitzGerald went so far as to contribute a question. Responsibility for the final version of questions and solutions are ours alone.

The project would not have been completed without the editing flair and publishing expertise of Helena Mulkerns.

We are particularly appreciative of the contributions of Deirdre O'Hanlon and Dorothy Scally who put in the hard yards, with remarkable fortitude, of typing the manuscript, proofing, and correcting the errors.

**Tim Bourke**
**William Scally**

# About the Authors

**Tim Bourke** worked as a senior executive in the agri-food sector and as a consultant in various areas of industry, together with educational and social research projects. He has also had a long term involvement in politics at academic, policy and grass roots level. An elite thinker, he passes much time observing and commenting on the machinations of humanity down the ages and across the continents. He enjoys nothing more than engaging with the great unknowns of the day. He delights in posing the abstruse question that requires an acrobatic mental agility to lead to the solution.

**William Scally's** working career spanned the semi-state corporate spectrum, the political arena, and working as policy adviser to various governments. He also worked as a public policy consultant and lecturer in adult education. A quintessential analyst and formidable interlocutor, he takes considerable pleasure in putting the knowledge quotient of family and friends on trial. That he has access to the solutions increases his enjoyment tenfold, as the quizzed strain their brains not alone to arrive at the answer but, frequently, to arrive at the very question.

www.TaraPress.net